Introducing Textile Printing

Introducing Textile Printing

Nora Proud

B T Batsford Limited   London

Watson-Guptill Publications   New York

© Nora Proud 1968

Published 1968 by B T Batsford Limited
4 Fitzhardinge Street London W1

Published 1968 by Watson-Guptill Publications
165 West 46th Street New York NY 10036

Reprinted 1969

Library of Congress Catalog Card Number 68-10202

Printed and bound in Denmark by F E Bording Limited   Copenhagen and London
7134 2415 ×

Contents

Acknowledgment

I acknowledge with grateful thanks the following who have helped in the preparation of this book:

Alan Dudley for all the photographs.

Peter Ross (11 years) and Keith Ross (16 years) who, as beginners in textile printing, have done most of the work illustrated.

Evelyn Samuel, Stephanie Bell, Norma Crockford, Margaret Thorne, Eric Dudley, for the rest of the illustrations.

Elizabeth Proud for critical and clerical help; and Thelma M Nye of B T Batsford Ltd for her constant help and co-operation.

Putney 1968   NP

Foreword

It is still the custom in some English country districts at Easter-time to hard-boil eggs in water containing onion skins or other natural dyes. By arranging leaves and flowers round an egg and tying them in with cotton, patterns can be boiled on to the eggshell, some strong, some weak, depending on how well the dye 'takes' to the shell.

In the early days of textile dyeing, people experimented with natural dyes on the natural fibres which were used for weaving fabrics, cotton and linen from plants, silk and wool from animals. They found that certain dyes which would, for instance, colour wool beautifully, would have no effect—would not 'take' at all—on cotton, and it was gradually realised that each sort of fibre needed its own dyes and dyeing treatment to colour it.

Printed patterns raised another problem. The dye, having been extracted from its source, had to be mixed with some sort of gum before it was printed on to the fabric. This gum kept the pattern in its shape without running or blurring while the fabric was undergoing the hot, wet treatment (usually steaming) necessary for fixing the dye into the fibres. Again it was found that each kind of dye needed a particular type of gum to be completely effective and to wash out of the fabric without leaving any unnatural stiffness after the pattern had been fixed.

Fabrics are woven for a particular purpose—furnishing or clothing—and any dyed or printed decoration put on them must be able to withstand whatever wear the cloth is likely to have. Curtains should not fade in sunlight, shirts and dresses should be unharmed by perspiration, and all must stand up to washing or cleaning.

Today all these problems are dealt with by the scientist. Although our textiles are woven, dyed and printed in factories, those people who want to design and print their own fabrics at home can now buy good dyes which are easy to use without special equipment.

Unlike dyeing processes, textile printing designs can always be tried out first on paper; the instructions given in the following pages should help the beginner to try his hand at designing and printing before he decides to invest in a set of dyes.

Practising an all-over printing rhythm

The first blocks used for printing were made from the bark of trees. Corks are made from bark. Use a cork to make your first prints.
You will need
    A flat plate, tin lid or wooden board
    A piece of thin foam rubber about 3″ × 3″
    A teaspoon or paint brush
    A thick pad of newspaper
    A small jar containing writing ink.

Using the spoon or brush, spread a little ink evenly over the foam rubber pad. Press the cork firmly two or three times on to the pad and then press it firmly on to the paper. Using a newsprint column as a guide, and working from left to right print a row of cork patterns touching each other (1). Continue printing another line under the first until you have made a square.

1 Printing with cork of thermos flask

Always press the block on the pad between each print or you will get uneven impressions.

If you are left-handed, print from right to left but always go down the page. In this way you are able to see where you are putting the print. Keep the board holding your pad and ink on the left of your work.

As you practise you will find you are able to keep your lines of print straight without a guide.

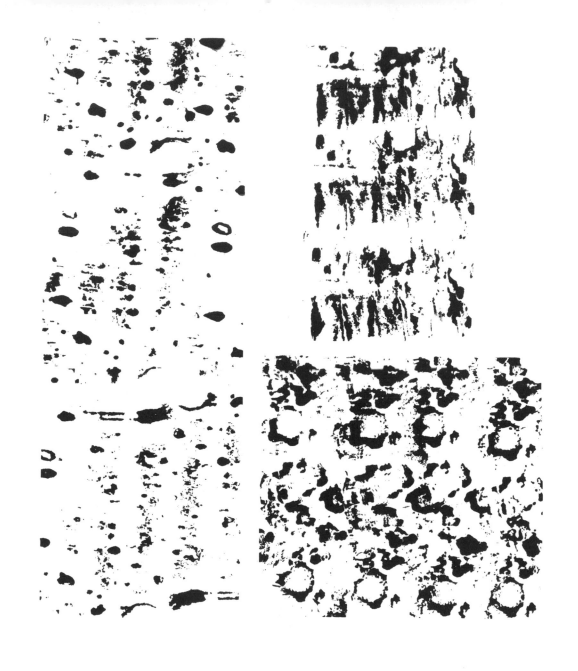

2 *Prints of different kinds of bark*

3   *Fir-cone prints*

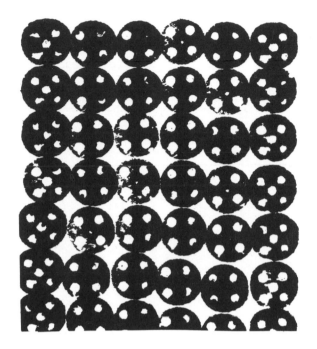

4   *Print of dice*

5   *Print of plastic toy wheel. Centre spots made with match-stick*

6 *Cotton-reel (spool) prints. The spots in the spaces between the prints were made with the end of a pencil*

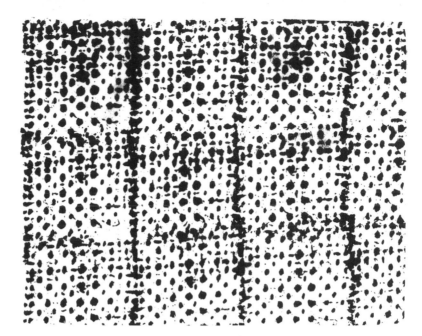

7   *Prints of small square of carpet underlay*

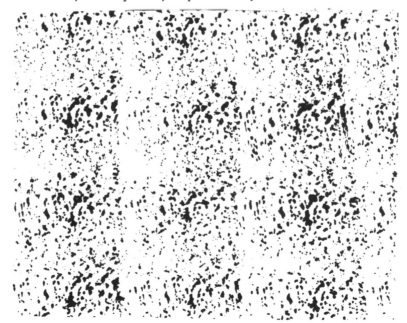

8   *Reverse side of 7*

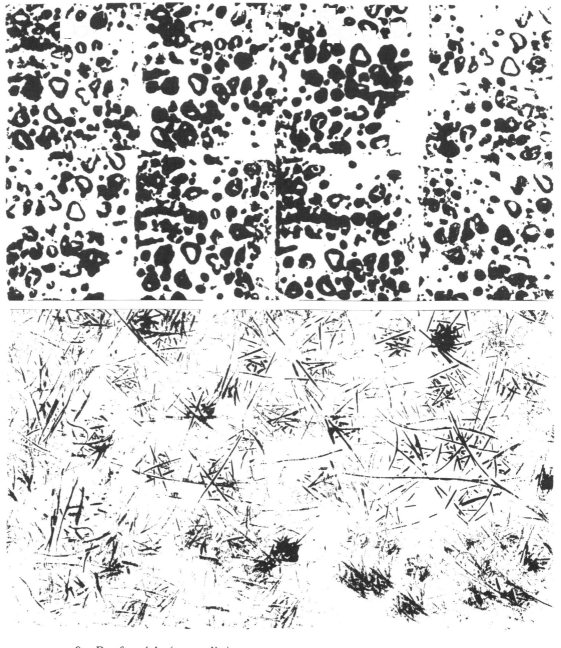

9   *Roofing felt (tarpaulin)*
10   *Fibreglass*

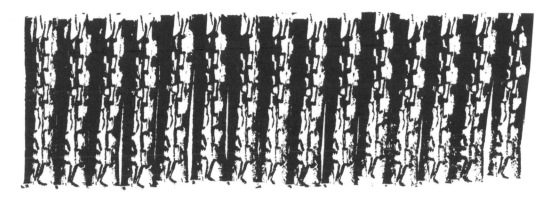

11   Corrugated cardboard edge

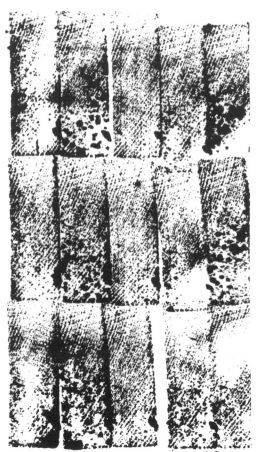

12   Edge of wood block

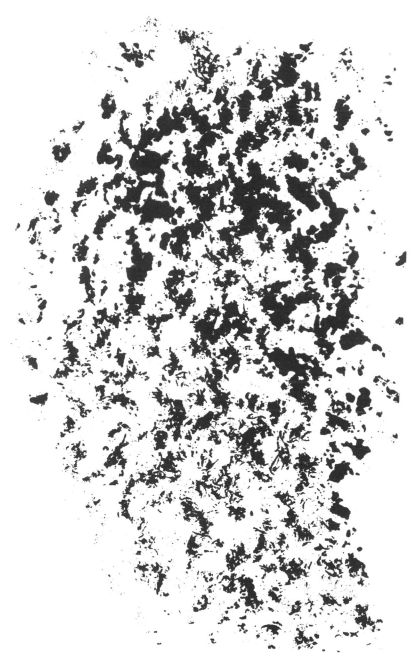

13   *Print of woven woollen fabric*   14   *Print of knitted woollen fabric*

15   Prints made from an apple cut in half

16　Prints made from an onion cut in half. The patterns in the spaces between the large circles are printed with a smaller slice of the same onion after layers have been peeled away

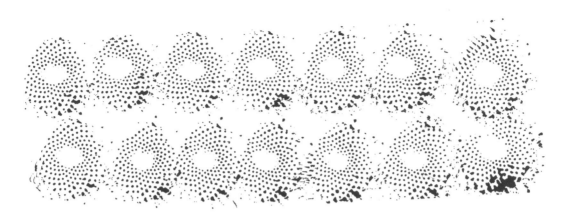

17   Marguerite after petals have dropped

18   Prints made with the underside of a toadstool

Mounting designs on blocks

You will find that some things would make good prints if they were easier to hold. Stick them on to an empty match-box, cotton-reel (spool) or block of wood.

You can begin to design more permanent blocks yourself by mounting, for example, pieces of string, rubber rings, and carpet underlay on small blocks of wood. Use an adhesive strong enough not to be loosened by ink or dye. Always keep the string, or whatever you are using to form the pattern, the same thickness.

19   Prints made from a leaf mounted on a piece of wood

Many of the natural things you try to print with will wear out very quickly, but they may give you some ideas for making your own patterns.

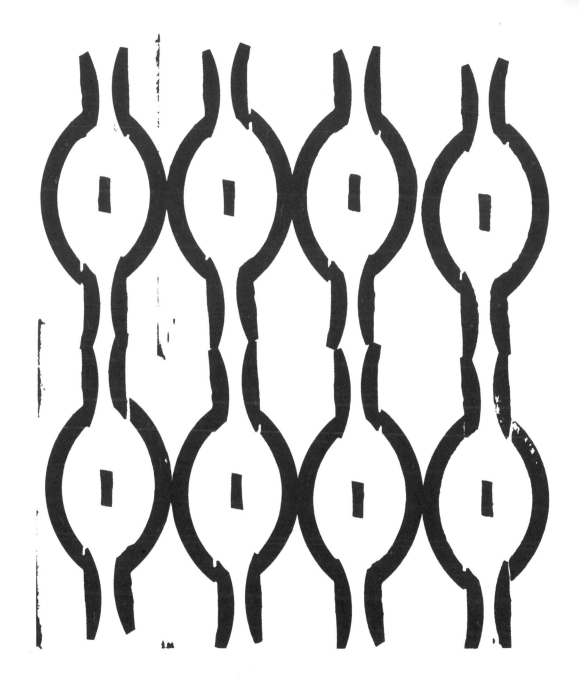

20   *Rubber jam jar rings cut and mounted*

21a

21b

21c

21a, b and c   Prints made from mounted string blocks

22 *Pattern of mounted match-sticks printed in red helizarin dye and blue spots printed with match-stick ends*

Spacing

When you are learning to play the piano, practising scales helps you to acquire the rhythm without which a piece of music would be meaningless. When you are learning to print fabrics your work will gradually become neater and quicker if you practise from side to side in rows with the prints touching each other. The spaces between the prints will be approximately equal and you may be able to improve your pattern by printing in the spaces, as in figure *6* (cotton-reels or spools) and figure *16* (onion).

As you become more experienced in designing you may want to leave more space between the prints. Decide how far apart you want them, mark off the intervals with a pencil along the top and bottom of your material, and crease it by folding as shown in figure *23*.

23

24   *Then mark off intervals down the sides of the material and crease by folding across*

Printing on cotton and linen fabric

You will need
  A flat plate, tin lid, or wooden board
  Pieces of thin foam rubber slightly larger than your biggest block
  A teaspoon or paint brush
  Newspapers
  An old piece of blanket, ironing sheet or piece of carpet underlay
    (if unobtainable a wad of newspaper will serve)
  Small containers (e.g. paste jars)
  Dye (see page 83 for information about dyes)
  Cleaning cloths
  Cotton or linen material.

Preparation of fabric

For first attempts at printing on fabric, old household linen (sheets and pillow-cases) is ideal. New material usually contains a stiffening substance known as 'dressing'. This dressing should be removed before printing by washing the material thoroughly so that the fibres will absorb the dye. Before you begin to print, iron the material to smooth any creases or roughness.

Spread your blanket on the table where you intend to print. Cover it with a sheet of newspaper to keep it clean. Put your fabric on this, and put your board holding foam pad, jar of dye, and block a little way away from the fabric on your right *(1)*. Print according to previous instructions. Be careful always to spread the dye very sparingly on the pad or your prints will be blotchy. Brush on more dye about every four or five prints.

Mixing of colours

On Plate I you will see that where the yellow shape is printed over the space between the red shapes, and overlapping them, the colour becomes orange. Where the blue spot is printed on the red shape it becomes more purple and where it is printed on the yellow shape it becomes green.

You can make mixed colours either by over-printing, as in Plate I, or by mixing them yourself before you begin to print.

It is a good idea when trying out new dyes to begin by mixing up separately small quantities of three primary colours: yellow, red, blue. In a fourth container mix a teaspoonful of the red mixture with a teaspoonful of the yellow mixture and make a row of prints with this orange until you have used it up. Then rinse the block, pad and container, dry them, and repeat the line of prints using a different combination of colours. From these three colours you should be able to mix orange, purple, green, grey, brown. See how many different colours you can make before you have used up all your dye.

Potato printing

You will need
 Printing equipment (page 33)
 Clean potatoes
 A large, sharp kitchen knife
 A wooden cutting board
 Gouging tools (lino-cutting nibs in holders are most suitable, but if you do not
  have these, pen nibs, small shells, or pen-knives make good substitutes).

Practise cutting potatoes. Slice the end of the potato off with your sharp knife, using a sawing action and pressing hard against the large part of the potato. This will ensure a smooth surface. Plate I shows a design printed with these simple potato shapes.

Alter the potato shape by slicing off the sides of the potato (as in figure 29b). Cut solid square, triangular, round, or oval shapes and make designs with these, practising over-printing in different colours as in Plate I and figure 26.

Make sure that you can always see the edge of your pattern area while you are printing, or you will not be able to place it correctly.

25 Potato print (spacing according to diagram 24)

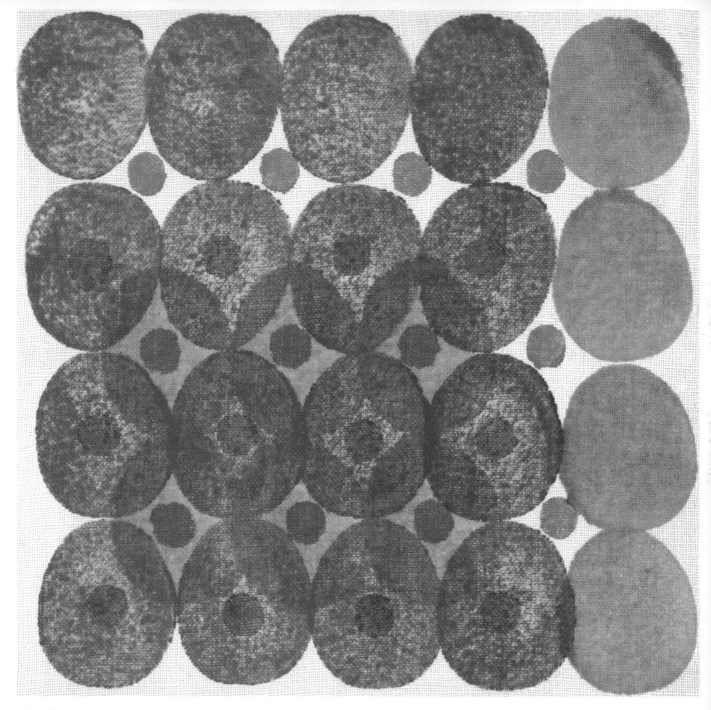

Plate I
Potato print on fabric showing over-printing with three primary or simple colours: red, blue and yellow

26　*Potato print in three colours: yellow, violet and red*

Always finish printing your design in one colour before starting with the next, or you will lose your rhythm and perhaps get into a muddle with your colours.

27a and b   Potato prints

Notice the shapes that are formed by the spaces between the prints.

28   *Design from two potato blocks*

The first print was a yellow diamond shape. A star pattern was gouged out of a long pointed shape and was printed in red over the yellow diamonds and the white spaces between.

29a   *Gouging negative pattern from potato surface with lino-cutting tool (Dryad no. 9 blade)*

29b   *Slicing off sides of potato to make an oblong block of 29*

30 The first of these patterns is printed with the block shown in 29 b. The second is from a block cut by

  1 printing 29 b on another potato surface (31 a and b)
  2 cutting away the coloured parts of the pattern (32) and making a positive form of 29 b, similar in idea to the negative and positive prints of a photograph

Look at 31a, b, c and d, and you will see the stages in cutting

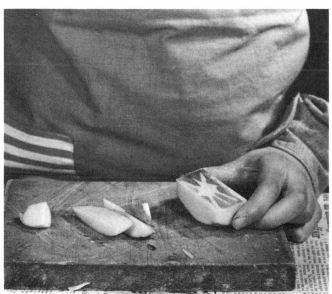

31a, b, c and d   Stages in cutting a positive pattern from a negative one

Plate II
Collage composed of plain and printed pieces of fabric stuck on to strong paper. Peter Ross

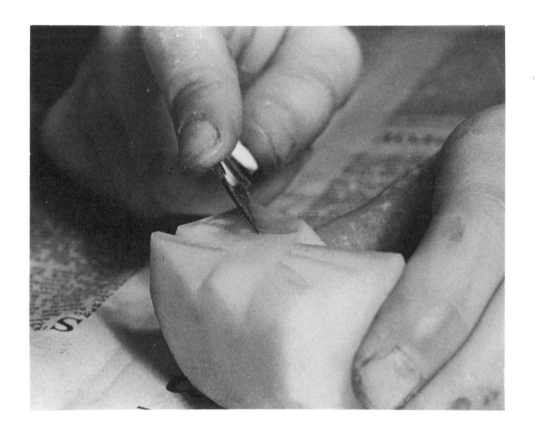

32   *You will need a small, flat blade (penknife or Dryad no. 5 blade) to cut this sort of pattern. Always cut into the potato diagonally away from the line that you want to preserve. This will make the line stronger for printing and will also make it easier to lift out the unwanted bits of potato*

33   Potato print. Block turned to form a larger pattern unit

You can form bigger pattern units by turning your block round. When you do this (as in figure *33*), finish one row of prints and then turn the block and print another row. In this way you keep a smoother rhythm. See also figure *37* for method of printing a pattern unit composed of four parts.

Lino blocks

Linoleum, or lino, is harder to cut than potato, but makes printing blocks that will last longer and wear better.

You will need

    Printing equipment (page 33)
    Pieces of lino
    Lino-cutting tools (especially Dryad no. 9)
    Flocking mordant
    Flocking powder
    Glass or perspex (Plexiglas) slab
    Rubber roller
    Turpentine substitute (for cleaning off flocking mordant).

Cut your design on the smooth surface of the lino in the same way that you gouged out your potato patterns *(29)*. The lino will be easier to cut if you warm it on a radiator or in front of a fire. Using strong glue, mount the lino design on a block of wood exactly the same size, and put it under a heavy weight until the glue sets. If you print with your block at this stage, you will get a textured print *(34)*.

34   *Lino print from unflocked block*

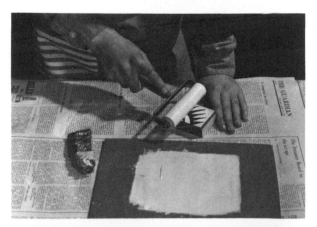

35a, b and c   Stages in flocking lino block

If you want a solid, even print, you must put a more absorbent surface on to the lino so that more dye will be picked up from the dye pad. This process is called 'flocking'.

Roll a little flocking mordant (about ½ in. for a small block) on to a glass slab until it is smooth and even. Then roll it on to the surface of the lino block, making sure that the edges and corners are all evenly spread (*35 a*).

Sprinkle flocking powder over the surface and gently spread it (*35 b* and *c*) until the white mordant cannot be seen. Again, pay special attention to the edges and corners. Leave to dry for 24 hours. Blow or brush off the surplus flocking powder and then the block is ready for use. Remember to wipe the glass slab and ruler with turpentine substitute as soon as you have finished flocking the block, otherwise the mordant will harden and be very difficult to remove.

Building up large designs
with one block

Lino designs can be cut on a much larger scale than potato patterns, obviously. It is possible, however, to build up larger designs and yet keep the even rhythm of printing with a block small enough to hold comfortably in one hand.

Figure *37a* shows how one carefully designed block, 2 in. square, may be used to print a larger pattern. First, with a ruler and pencil, mark off intervals across the top of the fabric, twice the breadth of the block, which must be square. In figure *37a* the marked intervals are at every 4 inches.

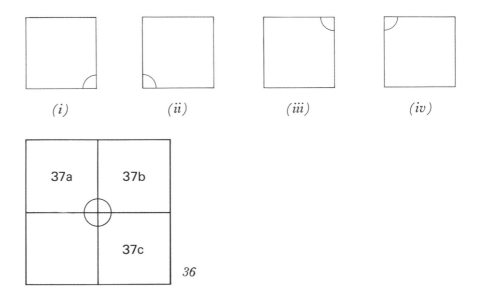

(i)　　　*(ii)*　　　*(iii)*　　　*(iv)*

36

Put a distinct pencil mark on the upper surface of the block across the corner which must always be the centre of the built-up pattern *(i)*.

Print the first row of pattern, placing the block carefully at each pencil mark *(37a)*.

Turn the block once, clockwise, so that the distinguishing mark is as at *(ii)* and complete the next row *(37b)*.

For row 3, turn the block twice in a clockwise direction, so that the distinguishing mark will be as at *(iii)* and print the second row so that each unit is three quarters complete; and for row 4 *(37c)* it will be as at *(iv)* and the first line of the pattern will be complete.

37a, b and c   Stages in printing pattern unit composed of four parts from one block

Building up circular designs

38

Circular designs can be built up by using a different rhythm of printing. Make a triangular potato block, fix the centre point of the design with a pencil, and print in the order shown in figure *38*.

Figures *39, 40* and *41* will give you some ideas for building up circular patterns.

39   Circular pattern built up with potato blocks

40   *Shuttlecock design*

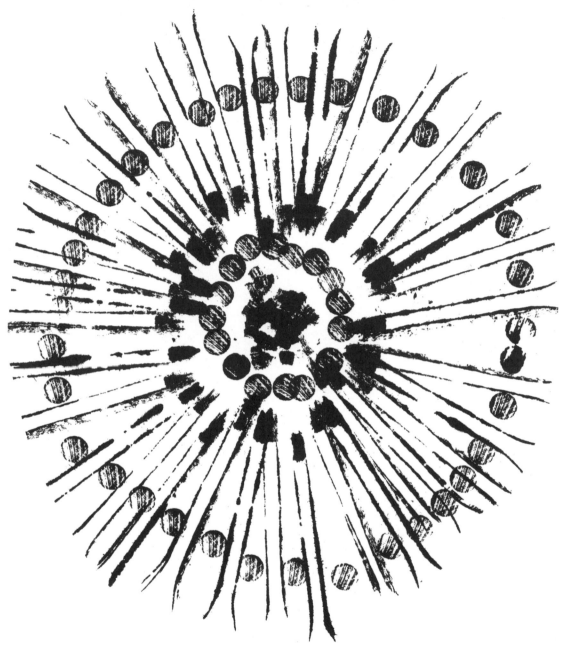

41 *Clothes-peg design in black and red. The spots were printed with the knob on the end of the peg and the line patterns with the side of the peg*

Polystyrene blocks

You will need
    Printing equipment (page 33)
    Polystyrene tiles or blocks
    A steel knitting needle
    A candle.

The characteristic texture of polystyrene shows very well in a print. It is possible also to burn patterns in the surface of a block of polystyrene. In figure *42* a pattern is being made in a polystyrene tile with the end of a steel knitting needle warmed in a candle flame. Figure *43* shows the resulting print.

42   *Burning a pattern in a polystyrene tile*

43   Print of 42

Planning a traycloth or place mat

As you learn how to print on fabric, you will want to make use of your work. If you want to make rectangular articles such as traycloths, table-cloths, these notes will help you to plan them without wasting material.

Cut your prepared fabric to the required size. Fold it carefully into four equal parts and press your finger gently along the folds to crease it. Open it out and spread it on your printing table. Begin printing in the lower right-hand angle, at the centre and continue until the lower right-hand quarter is complete *(44a)*. Turn your cloth round so that the printed part becomes the upper left-hand quarter and print the upper right-hand quarter, carrying on the previous rows of printing *(44b)*. When the upper half of the cloth is complete, continue the lines of printing all the way from left to right *(44c)*. Figure *44d* shows the finished cloth.

44a, b and c   Stages in printing a traycloth, beginning at the central point

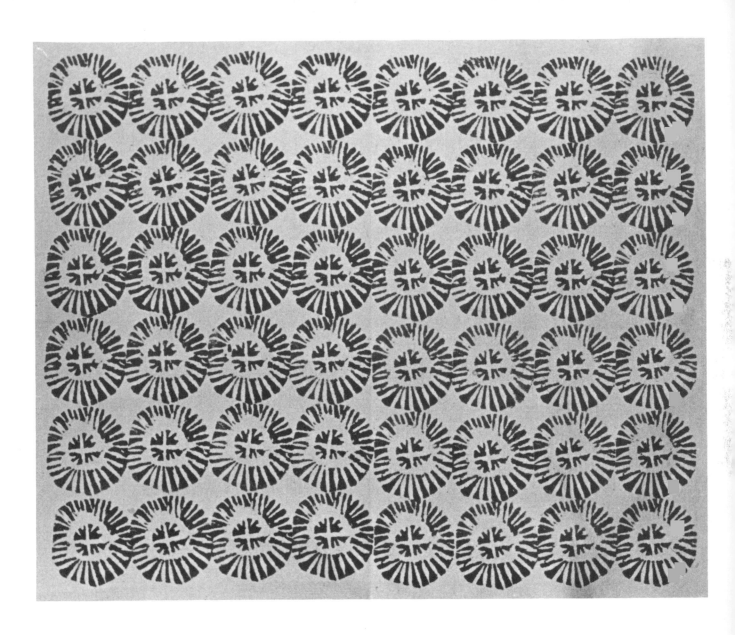

44d *Finished traycloth*

Printing borders and turning corners

Sometimes you will want to print borders on rectangular articles. Choose very simple patterns for these, as it is not easy to make the corners neat with elaborate border designs.

Cut your prepared material to the required size. Make a crease dividing equally each corner by folding *(45a)*. If a wide hem allowance is required, crease the material by folding along each side to mark where the border is to be printed. Place a piece of strong paper to cover the first half of the first corner and make your first print *(45b)*. In figure *45c* you will see that it has appeared half on the paper and half on the fabric. Continue printing. Just before you arrive at the second corner, cover the further half of it with a piece of paper before printing to the end *(45d)*. Turn your cloth in an anti-clockwise direction, place the paper over the printed half of the corner, and print the next side in the same way. Figure *45e* shows the last side being printed.

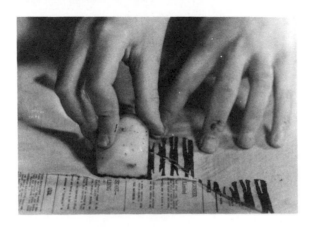

45a, b, c

45a, b, c, d and e   Turning the corners in printing a border on a traycloth

45f   Finished border on traycloth

Screen printing

Screen printing gives scope for a wider range of pattern-making than printing with blocks. The photographs on pages 67 to 71 will show you how to make a screen and try out simple patterns with it.

You will need

A wooden frame (the frame in figure *46a* is made from 2 pieces of wood 18″ × 1″ × ½″, and 2 pieces of wood 24″ × 1″ × ½″)

A squeegee or piece of rubber tile

Drawing pins (thumb tacks) or staple gun

Organdie muslin slightly larger than frame

A roll of gumstrip

A bowl of water

Candle wax or Marvin Medium (white glue)

A pencil and ruler

A paint brush

Scissors

A table covered with blanket or thin foam rubber

Newspapers

Dye

Cotton or linen fabric

Cleaning cloths.

46a   Pinning organdie muslin to frame

46b   Drawing round square board to make pattern area

Pin the organdie muslin to the sides of the wooden frame. Always start pinning at the centre and work to the corners, stretching it as evenly as possible while you are pinning *(46a)*. Wet the muslin all over and let it dry. This will shrink it slightly and make it taut.

Draw a square or a rectangle in the centre of the screen. This will be your pattern area *(46b)*.

46c   Lining screen with gumstrip, leaving pattern area open

46d   Applying hot wax to screen to make it dye-proof

Line the screen inside and out with gumstrip, leaving only the pattern area exposed *(44b)*. Try to avoid wrinkling the gumstrip.

Make the screen dye-proof by painting hot candle wax or Marvin Medium (white glue) smoothly over the gumstrip, inside and out *(46d)*.

When this is quite dry the screen is ready for use.

47a   Placing screen over newspaper pattern on fabric

Cut several squares of newspaper the size of the pattern area and cut or tear patterns in them. Iron your material thoroughly to remove any creases or roughness. Lay it on your prepared table. Place the screen with the pattern area directly over one of the newspaper designs on the fabric *(47a)*.

Pour in a stream of dye *(47b)* and draw it across the pattern area with a squeegee, pressing firmly all the while. If you have not got a squeegee, a piece of rubber tiling will serve the same purpose *(47c)*.

When you lift up the screen, the newspaper pattern will stick to the under surface of the muslin by suction. You can make several more prints with the same pattern before it becomes saturated with dye.

47b   Pouring dye into the screen

The first print may be indistinct as the muslin soaks up quite a lot of dye. If you practise for a while on newspaper sheets before printing on fabric, you will learn exactly how much dye is needed for each print.

If your pattern is a repeating one, you must make guiding lines on the screen and on the fabric to help you to place it correctly.

You can use other newspaper patterns for printing over the first one in different colours, as in block-printing, but on a larger scale.

There are many more ways of making patterns on screens which you can learn about from other books, if you like this way of printing.

47c Drawing rubber tile (squeegee) across pattern area to force dye through the screen

The first prints from the newspaper pattern can be seen on the right of the photograph.

Some ways in which
to use printed fabrics

As you learn more about pattern-making, and what sort of designs are suitable for certain purposes, you will plan your design and print your fabric for some use you have in mind. Small pieces of material that you print while you are experimenting can be used in various ways. The photographs in the next few pages may give you some ideas.

48　*Stocking doll in potato-printed dress　Girl 10*

49　*Glove puppet in cork-printed dress　Boy 6*

50   *Potato-printed shoe bag   Girl 10*

51 *'Stripey Cat'   Evelyn Samuel*
Potato-printed, washable soft toy

To make a soft toy, first cut a newspaper pattern. Remember to cut a piece for the base, around which you join the sides. Then your animal will stand up.

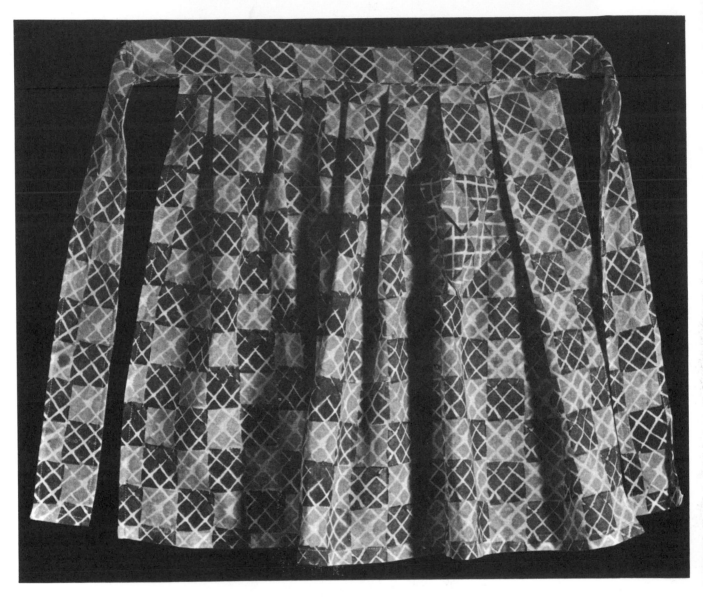

52   *Potato-printed apron   Girl 10*

53 *New potatoes have a finer texture than old ones. This design for a border was printed with carefully cut new potatoes*

54   Screen-printed tea towel   Norma Crockford

55 'Pappy's Tractor' Margaret Thorne

Decorative panel printed on cotton with corks, cotton-reels (spools) and potatoes

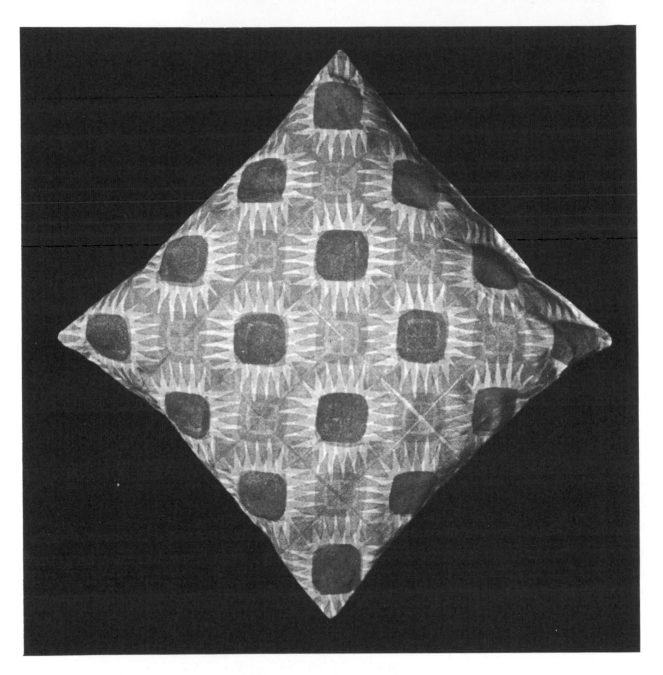

56   Cushion   Peter Ross   (see lino-print 37)

57   Detail from collage   Girls 13

Collage is a French word that is used to describe a picture composed of pieces stuck on to a foundation. In this case, the picture is composed of printed pieces of fabric stuck on to strong paper.

Information about dyes

Helizarin (*Acco-Lite* in the U.S.A.)

Helizarin and Tinolite are brand names of pigment dyes. These are very easy to prepare and to use and are made fast or fixed into the fabric by a simple heat treatment such as ironing. When used economically they make very little difference to the feel of the fabric, but can give undesirable stiffness if used carelessly.

The printing pastes are prepared in each case by mixing a little of the dye pigment into a white emulsion binder. They will keep for several weeks when mixed if they are kept in airtight jars. All containers, spoons and brushes should be washed in water immediately after use.

Procion

Procion (ICI) dyes can be used at home with excellent results but a little more preparation is required than for pigment dyes; a boiling treatment is necessary also to complete the dyeing process. The quality of the fabric when finished is superior to that printed with pigment dyes, and well worth the extra trouble involved.

Recipes are obtainable with the dyes.

Suppliers in Great Britain

Dyestuffs

Helizarin
Skilbeck Bros. Ltd, 55-57 Glengall Road, London SE15

Tinolite pigments and printing binder *CM*
Geigy (UK) Ltd, 42 Berkeley Square, London W1 and Simonsway, Manchester 22

Procion
Mayborn Products Ltd, 139-147 Sydenham Road, London SE26

Flocking mordant and powder, linoleum, lino-cutting tools, squeegee, organdie, muslin, *Brusho* (a water-colour powder economical for printing on paper), **rubber roller**

Dryad Handicrafts Ltd, Northgates, Leicester and 22 Bloomsbury Street, London WC1

Thin foam rubber

Most branches of Boots Chemists and Woolworths

Polystyrene tiles, rubber tiles, wood strips or blocks

General stores and Do-it-Yourself shops

Adhesives *(Bostik, Evostik, Cowgum)*

Most stationers and general stores

Marvin Medium
Margros Limited, Monument House, Monument Way West, Woking, Surrey

Suppliers in the USA

Dyestuffs

Acco-Lite pigment colors
American Crayon Company, Sandusky, Ohio

Procion (minimum 1 lb) *Lissapol*
Chemical Manufacturing Company, Madison Avenue, New York, NY

Water-color powder *(Brusho)*
American Art Clay Company, 1560 Polco, Indianapolis, Indiana

Flocking mordant powder
ICI Organics Incorporated, 55 Canal Street, Providence, Rhode Island

Linoleum
American Crayon Company, Division of the Joseph Dixon Crucible Company,
2002 Hayes Avenue, Sandusky, Ohio

Lino-cutting tools
Ontario Knife Company, 4151 Corbin, Franklinville, New York, NY

Linoleum blocks, linoleum cutters, rubber roller, squeegee, polystyrene, water-proof glue, water-color powder
Any good sized art materials supply store

Cotton organdie, flock, flocking adhesive, squeegee
Active Process Supply, New York, NY
Silk Screen Suppliers Inc, 32 Lafeyette Avenue, New York, NY
or any silk screen supply house

Rubber roller
Rapid Roller Company Ltd, 2556 S. Federal Street, Chicago 16

Bibliography

Textile Printing and Dyeing Nora Proud, *Batsford London and Reinhold New York*

Creative Print Making *(British edition)* Peter Green, *Batsford London*

New Creative Print Making *(U S edition)* Peter Green, *Watson-Guptill New York*

Print Making With a Spoon Norman Gorbaty, *Reinhold New York*

Printmaking Without a Press Janet Erickson and Adelaide Sproul, *Reinhold New York*

Linocuts and Woodcuts Michael Rothenstein, *Studio Vista London*

Print Your Own Fabrics Jutta Lammer, *Batsford London and Watson-Guptill New York*

Simple Printmaking Cyril Kent and Mary Cooper, *Studio Vista London and Watson-Guptill New York*

Surface Printing Peter Green, *Batsford London and Watson-Guptill New York*

Creative Textile Craft: Thread and Fabric Rolf Hartung, *Batsford London and Reinhold New York*

Colour and Texture in Creative Textile Craft Rolf Hartung, *Batsford London and Reinhold New York*

Printed Rag Toys Joy Wilcox, *Batsford London*

Index